Five reasons why love Mirabelle...

Mirabelle is magical and mischievous!

Mirabelle is half witch, half fairy, and totally naughty!

She loves making potions with her travelling potion kit!

Mirabelle loves sprinkling a sparkle of mischief wherever she goes!

She has a little baby dragon called Violet!

What would you like to see at a magical-creature sanctuary?

A butterphant, which is an elephant with butterfly wings!
– Samuel

A baby rainbow unicorn!
– Poppy

A giant two-headed puppy
with a big waggy tail.
– Lola

A big dragon that you
could ride.
– Iris

A magical fox with fire
for its tail.
– Rosie

A lightning sprite.
– Alex

The Loch Ness
monster!
– Harry

Family Tree

My Mum
Seraphina Starspell

My brother
Wilbur Starspell

My Dad
Alvin Starspell

Me!
Mirabelle Starspell

Violet

Illustrated by Mike Love, based on
original artwork by Harriet Muncaster

OXFORD
UNIVERSITY PRESS

Great Clarendon Street, Oxford OX2 6DP
Oxford University Press is a department of the University of Oxford.
It furthers the University's objective of excellence in research, scholarship,
and education by publishing worldwide. Oxford is a registered trade mark
of Oxford University Press in the UK and in certain other countries

Database right Oxford University Press (maker)

First published in 2022

British Library Cataloguing in Publication Data

Data available

ISBN: 978-0-19-277757-7

1 3 5 7 9 10 8 6 4 2

Printed in China

Paper used in the production of this book is a natural,
recyclable product made from wood grown in sustainable forests.
The manufacturing process conforms to the environmental
regulations of the country of origin.

From the world of ISADORA MOON

MIRABELLE

and the Naughty Bat Kittens

Harriet Muncaster

OXFORD
UNIVERSITY PRESS

Chapter ONE

It was a grey and gloomy Thursday afternoon at Miss Spindlewick's Witch School for Girls. Rain coursed down the arched windows of the classroom and I shivered with delight. I love a stormy ride home on my broomstick!

'Don't forget!' Miss Spindlewick said as we packed our bags. 'You must arrive on time tomorrow morning for the school trip. And make sure you wear sensible clothes!'

I hadn't forgotten. I had been looking forward to this trip for ages! We were going to a magical-creature sanctuary, deep in the forest. There were going to be all kinds of rescued magical creatures there that I had never seen before. The sanctuary looked after them until they were ready to be released back into the wild.

'I can't wait to see the broomstick-tailed goblin monkeys,' said my best friend Carlotta, as she zipped up her pencil case. 'They're going to be so cute!'

'I'm hoping there will be some bittens!' I said.

'Ooh, yes!' squealed Carlotta. 'I've never seen a real bitten before.'

'Me neither!' I said.

Bittens are bat kittens. Baby bat cats! They have large fangs, and bat wings so that they can fly. Bittens are much bigger than normal kittens and they always have black or purple fur. Sometimes striped. They are my favourite creature of all the ones we learned about this term, and I chose to do my entire project on them!

'I'm hoping there will be some giant spiders!' said a witch called Lavinia, from the back of the classroom. 'I looove creepy crawly spiders!'

I gave a small shiver. Most witches

are not afraid of spiders. In fact, they eat them on their toast for breakfast! But I am half witch and half fairy. I don't *mind* spiders (as long as they're not giant ones!) but I definitely don't like eating them! Everyone in my class knows that I bring a special lunchbox full of fairy food into school every day. Sometimes Lavinia goody-two-shoes teases me about it, but I don't care! Fairy honey sandwiches are much tastier than spiders on toast!

I was just zipping up my bag to go home when Miss Spindlewick called me over to her desk.

'Mirabelle Starspell!' she said. 'And Carlotta Cobweb. I'd like a word with you both before you leave the classroom please.'

My excitement about the trip sank like a stone inside my tummy.

'What have we done now?' I whispered to Carlotta, as the rest of the class filed out of the room.

Carlotta shrugged as we made our way over to Miss Spindlewick's desk.

'Maybe she noticed we were messing around in potions class this morning?' Carlotta whispered. 'You *did* accidentally turn your hands purple!'

I quickly put my hands behind my back.

'Or maybe it's because Violet and Midnight were play-fighting all through the spelling test this afternoon?' Carlotta said.

Violet is my pet dragon and Midnight is Carlotta's silky, black kitten. They love playing together, but sometimes they distract the class during lessons. Miss Spindlewick is always telling Carlotta and me to train our familiars properly.

'Oh . . . yes,' I said, biting my lip anxiously.

The room was empty now. Miss Spindlewick stood by her desk looking tall

and spiky and imposing. Her eyes were like two black, glittering currants blinking down at us. She didn't look pleased.

'Mirabelle Starspell and Carlotta Cobweb! The two of you together are *trouble*.'

'What?!' gasped Carlotta, trying to look innocent.

I didn't say anything. It *was* sort of true. Carlotta and I don't mean to cause trouble together, but sometimes we just get carried away and things *happen.*

'You think I don't see you messing around in potions class?' said Miss Spindlewick. 'Or doing sneaky loop-the-loops in the air during flying practice? Or letting your familiars roll around on the floor together during a spelling test?'

I stared down at the floor, blushing.

'Well, I do!' said Miss Spindlewick. 'I see you both!'

She stared at us hard with her dark, witchy eyes. I felt myself shiver. Where was Miss Spindlewick going with this?

Was she going to give us a detention?
Make us clean out all the dirty cauldrons
without magic?

'I am going to split you up!' said Miss
Spindlewick. 'Tomorrow, on the school trip,
you will both be partnered with different
witches.'

'No!' I cried before I could stop myself.

'But—' began Carlotta.

'No buts!' said Miss Spindlewick.
'Carlotta you will be paired with Hazel and
Mirabelle you will be partnered with . . .
Lavinia.'

'Lavinia?' I gasped.

'Yes,' said Miss Spindlewick, and I saw
her smile slyly. Miss Spindlewick *knows*

Lavinia and I don't get on!

'Lavinia will be a wonderful influence on you, Mirabelle,' she said. 'And there will be no chance of you and Carlotta causing mischief together.'

'*But!*' I began. '*Lavinia isn't any fu . . .*'

Miss Spindlewick glared at me and I trailed off, not daring to finish the sentence. Miss Spindlewick doesn't care about having fun. She's positively *allergic* to fun. So instead I gave a big sigh.

'So, I'll see you both tomorrow,' said Miss Spindlewick. 'Bright and early. Don't be late!'

Carlotta and I made our way out of school and into the playground. It was still raining and the sky was dark overhead. I had been looking forward to a wild and stormy ride home on my broomstick (though, sometimes, if the weather is *too* bad I have to wait for Mum and Dad to collect me in the car) but now I just felt dejected.

'The trip is going to be so boring now!' I said.

'I know,' said Carlotta. 'I was so looking forward to us going round the sanctuary together!'

'At least you're partnered with Hazel,' I said as I got onto my broomstick. 'She's all right. But *Lavinia!*'

The two of us rose into the air and waved goodbye to each other. I turned towards home, enjoying the feeling of the wind buffeting me up and down, despite my gloomy mood. It was like being on a rollercoaster! When I reached the edge of the forest I saw my brother, Wilbur, hovering in the air, waiting for me. He goes to wizard school and we always meet here on our way home.

'Hey, Wilbur,' I said unenthusiastically.

'What's up with you?' said Wilbur.

'Oh, it's nothing,' I said. 'We're

going to the magical-creature sanctuary

tomorrow and—'

'Oh, yeah!' said Wilbur. 'I'm SOOO jealous! I wish I was going on a school trip tomorrow! I know *everything* about magical creatures. Do you think there will be some star-spotted eels there? Or any moon unicorns? They only come out at night, you know, and they have a moon-shaped patch of fur on their foreheads. Ooh, and do you think they'll have some bittens? I've never seen a real bitten before.'

'Maybe,' I shrugged. There was no point telling Wilbur about Lavinia. He would never understand. And I couldn't get a word in edgeways anyway. He was going on and on, spouting all the facts that he knew about magical creatures—his latest obsession.

'I bet you don't know what a bitten's favourite thing *ever* is?' he asked annoyingly.

'Of course I do!' I said. 'I did my whole project on bittens this term.'

'What is it, then?' asked Wilbur.

'They *love* playing,' I said confidently.

'Yes,' said Wilbur. 'But what are their *favourite* things to play with?'

'They like chasing . . . bumblebees?'

'Wrong!' said Wilbur, delightedly. 'Most people think it's bumblebees, but if you do proper research it's *actually* butterflies. You can always distract a bitten with a butterfly.'

  25

'I *did* know that,' I lied. 'I just forgot.'

'What is a moon unicorn's favourite meal?' asked Wilbur.

'Um . . .' I began.

'Snafflegrass!' said Wilbur triumphantly, before I even had time to reply. 'Oh, I wish I was going to a magical-creature sanctuary tomorrow, instead of doing a boring spelling test!'

'I wouldn't be too jealous, Wilbur,' I said under my breath. '*I* won't be having much fun there.'

By the time I got home I was still feeling quite grumpy about the school trip, but I

cheered up when I saw that a package had
arrived for me.

'It's from your cousin, Isadora!' said
Mum.

I tore the package open. Inside there
were three new, sparkly hair clips: a
glittering shooting star, a bat with heart
eyes, and a butterfly with crystal-spotted
wings. There was also a postcard with a
picture of a beach on it.

'Those are pretty,' said Mum,
glancing over my shoulder.
'How nice of Isadora to
think of buying you a
present while she's on
holiday!'

27

'Yes!' I said, and felt a warm fuzzy feeling spread all the way through me. It felt nice to know that my cousin had been thinking of me.

I snapped all three hair clips into my hair and skipped into the kitchen to get an after-school snack. Maybe I would buy Isadora a present at the magical-creature sanctuary gift shop to say thank you tomorrow! The thought of that cheered me up even more, and I forgot all about my grumpiness over being partnered with annoying, goody-two-shoes Lavinia.

Chapter TWO

The following morning I woke up bright and early. It was the day of the school trip! I bounced out of bed and hurried to get dressed in my most practical clothes like Miss Spindlewick had told us to, but I couldn't resist putting just one of the hair clips that Isadora had sent me into my hair—the butterfly one. It wasn't very practical but it was so pretty! I raced downstairs and gobbled up my breakfast at super-quick speed. My excitement about going to the magical-creature sanctuary was back at full force!

'Slow down!' laughed Mum as she sipped coffee from her black cauldron-shaped mug. 'You'll give yourself a tummy ache! And you've got to wait for Wilbur before you can leave the house anyway.'

Mum and Dad let Wilbur and me fly to school on our own every morning as long as we stick together until we get to the edge of the forest.

'He had better not be late!' I said.

'Wilbur's never late for school,' said Dad, and I felt a small prickle of annoyance. My brother Wilbur is so *perfect.* Eventually, he came sauntering down the stairs, and I waited impatiently while he ate his breakfast and Dad made our packed lunches. Finally, we were ready to go.

'Have a lovely day, my witchlings!' said Mum, as she kissed us both goodbye.

'Stay out of mischief, Mirabelle!' said Dad.

When I arrived at school I saw my classmates, standing in a huddle on the playground tarmac. Miss Spindlewick was there, ticking names off on a clipboard. I almost fell off my broomstick when I saw her! She didn't look like Miss Spindlewick at all! She was wearing a pair of khaki trousers with lots of pockets on them and she had a large rucksack on her back.

'We need to be prepared for every eventuality,' I heard her

saying, as I landed on the ground and immediately gravitated towards Carlotta.

'Oh, no, Mirabelle!' said Miss Spindlewick when she saw me. 'You need to find your *partner.*'

I glanced ruefully at my best friend and then looked around for Lavinia instead. She was standing at the edge of the group with her arms crossed. Her hair was up in a very neat ponytail, and her clothes didn't have a single crease in them.

'Oh, er . . . hi, Lavinia,' I said, sidling up to her.

Lavinia looked at me, haughtily.

'*Mirabelle,*' she said.

I felt my excitement levels drop slightly.

Miss Spindlewick started to hand out a clipboard and a camera to each pair of witches.

'I'd better take care of those,' said Lavinia shooting her hand out to grab the clipboard and camera as soon as Miss Spindlewick handed them to us. She slid them into her backpack before I could get a proper look at them.

'You must all be *very* careful with the cameras,' ordered Miss Spindlewick. 'They are school property. You may use them to take photos of the animals. And the clipboards are for taking notes.

You will each be doing a presentation with your partner next week about everything you have learned at the magical-creature sanctuary. Right, are we all ready to leave?'

'Yes, Miss Spindlewick,' chorused the class.

'Good!' said Miss Spindlewick. 'Get onto your broomsticks then, witches! We will fly in neat, crocodile formation.'

Miss Spindlewick gave me a pointed look.

'And you must all *stay in your pairs,*' she said.

I sighed as we all rose into the air, following Miss Spindlewick. I could

see Lavinia flying right beside me from out of the corner of my eye. She had her nose pointed in the air and she looked very smug, sitting there on her polished, shiny broomstick, with not a twig out of place.

'You know, Mirabelle,' she said after we had been flying for a while. 'That hair clip you're wearing looks a bit out of place today. We're meant to be wearing practical clothes. Not *spangly and sparkly* accessories.'

I felt my annoyance rise.

'I don't see why it matters to you!' I said.

'We are supposed to be in *fully* practical clothing. You never follow the rules!'

I rolled my eyes.

'It will hardly get in the way of anything!' I said. 'And it was a present from my cousin! I want to wear it!'

Lavinia didn't reply for a few moments.

'Well . . .' she said finally. 'Just remember, Mirabelle, that we are representatives of Miss Spindlewick's Witch School for Girls. It's important that we behave *impeccably* at the magical-creature sanctuary today. I don't want you getting me into trouble.'

'I doubt I'll have a chance to,' I said through gritted teeth.

From a few rows back I could hear the sound of Carlotta laughing with Hazel and I felt a wistful pang.

Thankfully, Lavinia didn't say anything else for the rest of the journey.

We followed Miss Spindlewick in silence, over the dark, green forest, going deeper and deeper, until we finally reached a place where the trees became a bit sparser. Down below I could see some large cages and enclosures.

'Ooh,' I said, craning my neck to see if I could spot any of the animals.

Miss Spindlewick pointed her broomstick downwards, towards an official-looking building nestled among the trees and we all followed her, landing two by two. The building had two large glass doors at the front, with an arch over them that read 'ENTRANCE'.

'Now, witches,' announced Miss Spindlewick. 'You must all stay in your pairs as we go through the entrance and the gift shop. There will be plenty of time to buy things at the end of the trip.'

'Yes, Miss Spindlewick,' we all chorused.

Miss Spindlewick pushed open the doors and went over to the counter to buy our tickets. We stood behind her in neat pairs and I gazed around in excitement. I *love* gift shops. They are almost my favourite part of going on a school trip. All around us were shelves of toy creatures. I could see a soft and squishy broomstick-tailed goblin monkey, a furry dragon with sequinned wings, and the most adorable, velvety bitten.

I wanted one of those for myself, very
badly. But I *had* promised myself I would
buy Isadora a present at the gift shop,
and I knew she would really love one, too.
Would I be able to afford two? I needed to
know! Miss Spindlewick was busy talking
to a wizard with a long beard behind the
counter. She probably wouldn't notice
if I just hopped out of the queue for a
tiny moment. I lifted my foot, preparing
to skitter over to the shelf while Miss
Spindlewick's back was turned when I felt
someone grab hold of my arm.

'Where are you going?' hissed Lavinia.
'Miss Spindlewick told us to stay in line!'

'I just wanted t—' I began.

'Already breaking rules!' said Lavinia. 'If you get into trouble then *I'll* get into trouble.'

'No, you won't . . .' I said but stopped when I saw the expression on Lavinia's face. She looked more than just a little worried. She looked *intensely anxious*.

'Don't worry, Lavinia,' I said, stepping back into line. 'I won't get you into trouble.'

Chapter THREE

I gazed longingly at the cuddly bittens
as we left the gift shop and exited the
building. Now we were standing at a sort
of crossroads. There was a big wooden
sign stuck into the ground that had arms
pointing in all directions, showing visitors
the way to all the different animals.

'I want to see the glow snakes first!' I

heard Hazel say to Carlotta.

'I want to see the cauldron-bellied fish!' said another witch called Kira.

'I want to see the star-spotted eels!' said someone else.

Miss Spindlewick called for silence.

'You all have one hour to start going around the sanctuary,' she said. 'And then we will meet back here for lunch. Remember to take notes and use the cameras to take photographs. And, most importantly, stay in your pairs! We are here to learn, and I don't want you getting distracted. Right, off you go, witches!'

I waved sadly at Carlotta as she disappeared off with Hazel in the direction of the glow snakes and then I turned back to Lavinia.

'Shall we go and see the bittens first?' I said. 'I do reeeally want to see them!'

Lavinia looked at me snootily.

'The *bittens* are right at the bottom end of the sanctuary,' she said. 'We may as well start with something closer. *I* want to see the giant spiders. They're in the opposite direction. Let's go there first.'

'Ugh!' I thought. The giant spiders were the *last* creatures I wanted to look at. But I didn't want to cause an argument with Lavinia this early in the day, so I traipsed after her as we made our way towards the giant spiders.

'Aren't they just so elegant!' said Lavinia, as we arrived at the spider enclosure and peered in. The enclosure was a very large cage covered in sticky webbing, with plenty of room for the spiders to scuttle around and play in. The spiders looked happy, and I *supposed* I could see what Lavinia meant by them being elegant, but I still couldn't help shuddering at their size. They were so big!

Some of them were bigger than me! And they all had huge fangs.

Lavinia handed me the clipboard.

'You take notes,' she ordered. 'I'll take the photos.'

Lavinia began to snap away with the camera while I chewed the end of the pencil and wondered what to write about the spiders. In the end, I wrote: BIG AND HAIRY.

'You need to write more than that,' said Lavinia, bossily. 'Let me dictate.'

'Why don't *you* write and *I'll* take pictures?' I suggested. Taking the photos looked like fun!

'I don't think that's sensible,' said Lavinia. 'You might drop the camera and then we'll get in trouble.' Hurriedly, she stowed the camera away in her backpack.

I rolled my eyes.

'I won't *drop* it.' I said.

'You might,' said Lavinia. And there was that fearful look on her face again!

'Why are you so worried about getting into a little bit of trouble?' I asked.

'I'm not,' she snapped. 'Why are you *never* worried about getting into trouble?'

I shrugged.

'I don't *like* getting into trouble,' I said. 'I don't do it on purpose! Well, mostly, I don't. But somehow I always seem to get into erm . . . scrapes.'

'You don't do it on purpose?' asked Lavinia.

'Not *all* the time,' I said. 'But I seem to get into trouble anyway. So what's the point of worrying about it?'

'Oh.' said Lavinia, and she looked a little shocked. '*I* thought you were always naughty on purpose.'

'I mean I am *sometimes*,' I admitted, feeling myself blush. 'I just like having fun.'

'Hmm, I see,' said Lavinia, and her expression became a little less haughty. 'Shall we go and look at the bittens now? You said you wanted to.'

Lavinia and I made our way through the forest towards the bottom of the magical-creature sanctuary where the bittens were kept. On the way, we passed the moon unicorns and the dragons, which we stopped and looked at. Lavinia gave me the clipboard again while she snapped the photos. It was so annoying. Finally, we reached the bittens and I clasped my hands together and squealed when I saw them. They were so adorable. Some of them were fluttering around their enclosure on their big leathery, bat wings, some were play-fighting on the ground, and some were curled up asleep in a basket. Their fur looked so smooth and silky and they all had such big beautiful, purple cat eyes. Like amethysts!

'I love them!' I cried.

'They *are* pretty cute,' agreed Lavinia.

'Please, let me have the camera!'

I said. 'I want to take photos. Bittens are my favourite!'

'*I'll* take the photos,' insisted Lavinia.

I started to feel very annoyed then.

'You've taken all the photos so far!' I said. 'It's my turn.'

'I told you, I don't trust you with the camera,' said Lavinia, getting it out of her rucksack and holding onto it tight. 'Just let me do it.'

I felt angry tears spring to my eyes. Lavinia was being so unfair!

Lavinia lifted the camera to her face and put her eye to the viewfinder. Without thinking, I reached out and tried to grab it. It was *my* turn!

'Hey!' shouted Lavinia, pulling it back.

We tussled for a few moments,

Lavinia's face turning tomato red. Then I gave one almighty tug and Lavinia tugged back, and suddenly the camera went flying out of both our hands, through the narrow bars of the bitten enclosure.

'Mirabelle!' gasped Lavinia and suddenly tears sprung to her eyes too. 'Look what you've done!'

Chapter FOUR

'It wasn't *just* me!' I said, staring in horror at the camera which was now lying right by the bittens' basket. It was too far away for me to be able to grab it. The bittens all scampered over to it, sniffing and licking it, very interested in this new thing that had appeared in their enclosure.

'Miss Spindlewick will be so cross!'

wailed Lavinia. 'What are we going to do?'

Then she burst into tears. 'I've never been in trouble with Miss Spindlewick before!' she said. 'Never!'

'Oh,' I said, thinking back to her worried face. Now it all made sense. Lavinia was Miss Spindlewick's star pupil. The expectation to be perfect all the time must feel like a lot of pressure. I couldn't help feeling a *tiny* bit sorry for her.

'It's OK,' I said, reaching out my hand to pat her arm. 'We'll get it back and Miss Spindlewick will never know!'

'But *how*?' said Lavinia.

'We'll do a spell to unlock the gate,' I said. 'I'll slip in and grab the camera, and then I'll lock the gate again. No one will know!'

'A spell to unlock the gate?' gasped Lavinia. 'That would be *really naughty*!'

'I know,' I said. 'But Miss Spindlewick never has to know. Would you rather leave the camera there and get into trouble?'

Lavinia stared at me, her face pale.

'No,' she whispered.

'Then let's just do a quick spell,' I said.

'But I didn't bring any potion ingredients,' said Lavinia. 'I didn't *expect* to have to do a spell!'

'That's OK,' I said. 'I've got emergency potion ingredients with me! You never know when you might need to get out of a . . . situation.'

I reached into my top and pulled out a necklace that had a row of tiny bottles on it. Lavinia stared at it in admiration.

'That's brilliant!' she said.

I took the necklace off and let her look at it. She gazed at the tiny bottles for a while before saying, 'Crushed moonrock and powdered bat's claw should do it. We can mix them up in the lid of my flask.'

Together we opened the tiny, potion bottles and poured the ingredients into the lid of Lavinia's flask, mixing them up with a twig that we found nearby.

'You chant the spell,' I said to Lavinia. 'You always get top marks in potions class. It's got more chance of going right if you do it.'

'OK,' said Lavinia, 'But you have to promise you won't tell Miss Spindlewick that I've done a secret spell.'

'Of course, I won't!' I said, shocked. 'I'm not a tell-tale!'

Lavinia smiled at me and I swore I could see tiny sparkles of excitement dancing in her eyes. Then she started to chant:

Claw of bat and dust of rock,
Help us to unpick this lock,

Lavinia mixed the two potion ingredients up together, dropping in a bit of water from her flask to bind them together. Now it looked like a sort of purple paste with glittering flecks in it.

'You do the rest!' said Lavinia, pushing the lid of the flask towards me. 'I don't dare!'

I took the potion over to the enclosure and scooped a bit of it out with my finger, rubbing it onto the padlock. Immediately I heard a click.

'It's open!' I said.

Feeling my heart begin to race inside
my chest, I looked around to check no
one was around. Then I opened up the
gate and slipped inside, hurrying over to
fetch the camera as quickly as I could. The
bittens scampered over to me, their big
amethyst eyes gazing up at my hair.

'Hurry, Mirabelle!' hissed Lavinia from outside the gate. 'Before anyone comes!'

I picked up the camera and slipped back out of the gate, closing it behind me. I was just in time!

'Lavinia! Mirabelle!' came Miss Spindlewick's voice as she came strolling around the corner. 'How are you getting on?'

'Fine, Miss Spindlewick!' I squeaked, knowing my face had turned red. I suddenly felt incredibly guilty. I felt like Miss Spindlewick would be able to see exactly what I'd just done. But she just smiled and nodded at us both before peering into the bittens' cage and then continuing on her way.

Lavinia and I both looked at each other and breathed a sigh of relief.

'That was close!' I said.

'Too close!' agreed Lavinia. 'But at least we've got the camera back now! And all thanks to you, Mirabelle!'

'Oh, well . . .' I said. '*You* did the spell!'

'But *you* had the ingredients for it,' said Lavinia. 'And you snuck into the cage. I would never have dared to do that! Thank you, Mirabelle! I'm so relieved we won't get into trouble!'

'That's OK, Lavinia.' I smiled. 'It was teamwork!'

It felt nice to be getting on well together for the first time ever! After I had snapped a few photos of the bittens, Lavinia looked at her watch.

'We have to get back to the group,' she said. 'It's lunchtime!'

Lavinia and I hurried back to the entrance where the rest of our class was waiting, all chattering excitedly. Miss Spindlewick ticked names off on her clipboard. Then she led us to an outdoor area where there were lots of benches and tables. I started heading towards Carlotta—surely Miss Spindlewick would let me sit next to my best friend for lunch? But Lavinia pulled me back.

'Here's a good spot, Mirabelle,' she said, pointing to an empty table.

'Oh!' I said. 'I . . .'

'Come on, Mirabelle,' she said. 'Sit down!'

I dithered for a moment. It almost felt like Lavinia wanted to sit next to me at lunch today. And I didn't want to hurt her feelings. Gazing wistfully over at Carlotta, I sat down next to Lavinia and opened my lunchbox. Dad had made me my favourite sandwiches, with fairy honey inside them.

There was an apple, and a blossom-nectar yoghurt, too, along with some rose-petal-flake crisps. I glanced sideways at Lavinia, expecting her to tease me for eating fairy food like she usually does, but she didn't say anything, she was busy tucking into her slug sandwich.

Ugh! I thought, shuddering. Usually,
I would tease Lavinia back about her
witchy lunch, telling her how disgusting
I thought it was. But, strangely, today
I didn't feel like it. Instead, we started
talking about all the animals we had seen
so far that day. It felt rather nice.

Suddenly, there was a loud squeal
from a few benches away.

'*Carlotta!*' Hazel yelled.

I craned my neck to see Hazel jumping up and down, shaking her clothes.

'What's going on?' asked Miss Spindlewick from her table.

'Carlotta poured her Spider Frizzles down my top!' shouted Hazel, crossly.

I could see Carlotta trying not to laugh and I pressed my lips together, trying not to laugh, too.

'Carlotta Cobweb!' snapped Miss Spindlewick. 'That is not appropriate behaviour, as you well know! You will spend the rest of the day going around the magical-creature sanctuary with *me*!'

Carlotta gasped.

'But Miss Spindlewick!' she cried. 'It was just a joke! It was supposed to be funny!'

'Well it's not very funny for Hazel, is it?' said Miss Spindlewick. 'Hazel, you may join up with Kira and Tabitha for the rest of the day. Carlotta, come and sit next to me, please.'

I saw Carlotta sigh as she gathered up her lunchbox and traipsed over to Miss Spindlewick's table. Poor Carlotta!

'Poor Hazel,' said Lavinia.

'Mmm,' I said. Now that I thought about it, I did feel a bit sorry for Hazel. It *wasn't* really very kind of Carlotta to pour Spider Frizzles down her top. I watched Carlotta sit down next to Miss Spindlewick at the table and for the first time, I felt just a tiny bit glad that we hadn't been partnered together today. It was nice to not be in trouble for once!

I was halfway through my sandwiches, feeling good for staying out of mischief when there came a crackling sound

overhead, and suddenly a loud voice
boomed through one of the loudspeakers,
making me jump.

'WARNING. BITTENS ARE ON
THE LOOSE!'

Chapter FIVE

I almost choked on my sandwich. Lavinia stared at me.

'Mirabelle?' she said accusingly.

'What?' I replied, starting to panic. 'It wasn't me!'

Lavinia didn't look like she believed me.

'I *swear*!' I said. 'I didn't let them out. Not on *purpose* anyway!'

I put my sandwich down, suddenly feeling quite sick.

'Did you lock the door?' whispered Lavinia. 'When you came back out of the cage?'

'I thought I did!' I said, screwing my eyes tightly shut to try and remember. I came out of the bittens' cage and . . . Miss Spindlewick had suddenly appeared, and it startled me! Maybe I got distracted and forgot to snap the padlock back shut. 'Oh, no!' I said, with my head in my hands.

'THE BITTENS ARE ON THE LOOSE!' came the voice from the loudspeaker again. 'IF YOU SEE AN ESCAPED BITTEN, PLEASE REPORT

TO THE OFFICE, RIGHT AWAY.'

Miss Spindlewick stood up and gazed around at us all with her eyes narrowed.

'Who here knows anything about the escaped bittens?' she asked, in a stern voice.

I found myself shrinking back in my seat, then I started to put up my hand, but Lavinia pulled it back down.

'Don't tell her!' she hissed. 'We'll get into so much trouble. Please, Mirabelle! Let's find the bittens ourselves! It can't be too hard!'

I bit my lip. Lavinia looked SO frightened.

'OK . . .' I whispered.

'*Hmmm,*' said Miss Spindlewick, as she stared around at us all with suspicious, beady eyes. 'Well, we can all at least help to try and find the lost bittens. Pack up your lunches, witches, and go and search in your pairs! If you find a bitten, report to the office right away!'

'Yes, Miss Spindlewick,' we chorused, as we all packed away the rest of our

lunches and jumped up from our seats.

'Come on!' said Lavinia, tugging on my arm.

Together, Lavinia and I headed back into the magical-creature sanctuary, grabbing our broomsticks from the office on the way. From my research, I knew bittens liked hiding and climbing, so maybe they were high up?

'We should have a look in the treetops!' I suggested. So Lavinia and I flew upwards and peered in through the dark, leafy tops of the trees. But we couldn't see any bittens.

'I feel so guilty!' I said as we hovered in the air. 'What if the lost bittens are

never found?'

'I'm sure they will be,' said Lavinia. 'We have to stay positive!'

We flew around the tops of the trees for a little longer, and then we landed back down on the ground, keeping our eyes peeled as we walked along.

'I can hear chattering!' said Lavinia after a few moments.

'Me too,' I said.

We hurried around the corner of one of the enclosures and saw a gaggle of witches and wizards gathered beneath a large tree. Miss Spindlewick was there, with Carlotta and a few of our other classmates. They were all gazing up at the sky. I squinted and looked up, too. Fluttering around the tree were all the bittens, flapping their bat wings. They were swooping and soaring and loop-the-looping.

'They're found!' I cried, feeling my whole body relax with relief.

'Yes,' said Miss Spindlewick. 'Thank goodness!'

'STAND BACK EVERYONE!' came the voice of a keeper who had suddenly appeared in the sky on his broomstick, holding a very large net. 'THIS IS A DELICATE OPERATION.'

He whizzed up to the top of the tree, slowing down a little when he got close to the bittens. Immediately they zipped away from him, their little velvety tails wiggling in the air. Cautiously, the keeper flew a bit closer, gently swishing his net, but the bittens scooted away. Down below him, we all laughed. The keeper was starting to look flustered.

'Bittens are quick things,' I heard Miss Spindlewick say. 'He'll be lucky to catch them without a chase!'

'Maybe we should all try and help!' I suggested.

'Don't even think about it, Mirabelle Starspell!' said Miss Spindlewick. 'Leave it to the professionals.'

We watched for a while longer as the keeper continued to try and catch the bittens in his big net. But every time he came close they fluttered away. The keeper was starting to look a bit cross, and the bittens were showing no signs of stopping their game. I knew from doing my project that bittens can play for hours and hours.

They love chasing! And they especially love chasing butterflies . . . *butterflies!*

I reached up to touch my hair clip as a brilliant idea suddenly wooshed into my head. The bittens had been very interested in my hair when I had been in their cage, hadn't they? Maybe it was my butterfly hair clip they had been interested in, not my hair!

'Miss Spindlewick I have an idea!' I said, gripping hard onto my broomstick. 'Let me fly up there and—'

'Absolutely not!' said Miss Spindlewick.

'But . . .' I began. 'I think—'

'You'll stay right down here on the ground,' said Miss Spindlewick, and she held out her hand for my broomstick. Sighing, I reluctantly handed it over to her.

'Miss Spindlewick,' I tried again for the third time.

'Enough!' said Miss Spindlewick.

Slumping my shoulders, I moved a few steps away. I can't stand Miss Spindlewick sometimes!

'What's your idea?' whispered Lavinia. I looked up, surprised that she had followed me, and even more surprised that she was interested in my idea.

'Butterflies!' I whispered back. 'Bittens love butterflies! I'm sure I could lure them back into their enclosure with my butterfly *hair clip*. If Miss Spindlewick would let me . . . She's taken away my broomstick!'

'Oh!' said Lavinia. She stared down at her own broomstick, which she was holding in her hand. Then she looked up at the sky where the keeper was whirling around on his broomstick, now wildly waving his net about in the air. His face had gone bright red with the effort of trying to catch the bittens.

'You can use my broomstick if you like,' whispered Lavinia.

'Really?!' I gasped, shocked.

Lavinia nodded.

'I think your idea could work,' she said. 'I know Miss Spindlewick will be cross, but the most important thing is that the bittens are returned safely to their enclosure.'

'I know,' I said.

'Here,' said Lavinia, thrusting her broomstick towards me. 'Take it! Before I change my mind.'

I glanced at Miss Spindlewick, who was busy looking up at the sky, and then I grabbed Lavinia's broomstick.

'Mirabelle Starspell!!' I heard Miss Spindlewick yell, as I shot up into the air in front of everyone and whizzed over to where the bittens were tumbling about playfully in the sky.

'Come back down, please!' roared the keeper when he saw me. 'You'll disturb the delicate operation!'

I ignored both of them.

I was going to be in big, BIG trouble after this.

I took the hair clip out of my hair and held it out towards the bittens. As soon as they saw it they fluttered towards me, trying to bat at it with their paws.

I heard the crowd gasp.

'You can't catch the butterfly!' I teased, as I zipped away from the bittens holding my hairclip, heading in the direction of the enclosure. The bittens fluttered along playfully behind me, trying to catch it. I flew faster, waving my hair clip wildly about so that the gems glittered and twinkled in the light.

'Mew, mew, mew,' went the bittens, as they followed along behind me in a line. I did a loop-the-loop and then swooped down towards their enclosure, throwing the hair clip through the wide-open door. The bittens followed it in, tumbling over each other to be first to catch the butterfly.

I landed on the ground and quickly closed the door of their enclosure, just as the keeper arrived breathlessly on the ground beside me, and a crowd of witches and wizards who had been watching came running around the corner. When they spotted all the bittens back in the enclosure they let out a big cheer.

'Well done, Mirabelle!' said Lavinia. 'You did it!'

'Oh well . . .' I said. 'I couldn't have done it without you lending me your broomstick!'

Lavinia shot me a shy smile, and Miss Spindlewick arched her eyebrows in surprise.

The keeper locked the door to the bittens' enclosure tightly and scratched his head.

'I can't think *how* they all managed to escape,' he muttered. 'It's a real mystery!'

I felt myself go red and saw Miss Spindlewick give me a very suspicious look. I shuffled my feet, ready to tell

her everything, even if it meant getting told off in public. But before I could say anything, the keeper exclaimed, 'It was a GENIUS idea of yours to use your hair clip, young witchling! You're a credit to your school!'

Miss Spindlewick's furious expression softened a little.

'Well,' she said primly. 'Miss Spindlewick's Witch School for Girls *is* a very fine establishment. And Mirabelle, I'm pleased to see you've done your research on bittens.'

Lavinia and I spent the next hour going around the rest of the sanctuary together, taking it in turns to take photos of all the magical creatures. Now that we understood each other a little better, being partnered together actually turned out to be quite . . . fun!

Chapter SIX

At the end of the afternoon, we were
all allowed to spend some time in the
gift shop. I raced over to the cuddly-toy
bittens and looked at the price tag. Yes!
I was just able to afford two of them. One
for me and one for my cousin Isadora!
I spent ages looking at their faces,
deciding which ones looked the friendliest.

Finally, I chose two and brought them over to the counter to pay for them. I felt so excited about sending my cousin such a lovely present. I knew she would love the toy bitten just as much as I loved the hair clips, though I did feel a bit disappointed that I had lost the butterfly one in the bittens' cage.

'What are you buying, Lavinia?' I asked her, as she came to stand next to me at the counter.

'Oh, just this!' she grinned, waving a horrid rubbery spider in my face.

The broomstick ride back to Miss
Spindlewick's Witch School for Girls
seemed much longer, now that we were
all tired from a full day at the magical-
creature sanctuary. Lavinia and I flew side
by side, chatting and laughing about our
day. I wondered if we would stay friends
once we got back to school, or whether

things would go back to how they had always been.

When we eventually landed on the playground tarmac, Miss Spindlewick ticked off all our names on her clipboard.

'Despite one small incident today,' she said, looking pointedly at me, 'I think we've all had a rather good trip, haven't we?'

'Yes, Miss Spindlewick,' we chorused.

'Good!' smiled Miss Spindlewick. 'Well, it's the end of the day so you're all free to fly home!'

I waved at Carlotta and gathered up my broomstick, about to hop onto it when I felt someone pulling at my elbow. It was Lavinia.

'Mirabelle,' she said. 'I bought you something in the gift shop.'

'Me?' I said, shocked. I really hoped she wasn't going to give me that nasty, rubbery spider.

'Yes,' said Lavinia. 'To say thank you for being my partner today. It was much more fun than I had imagined!'

She reached into her pocket and pulled out a hair clip.

'To replace the one you lost,' she said.

I took the hair clip and gazed at it, and a warm feeling spread all the way through my body. It wasn't a butterfly hair clip, but a small bitten-shaped one, with glittery bat wings.

'Oh, I LOVE it!' I said, jumping on
top of Lavinia and giving her a huge hug.
'Thank you so much!'

'You're welcome,' said Lavinia,
sounding a bit embarrassed. 'I just
thought it was nice of you to . . . Well, you
know, get the camera back for us so that

we didn't get into trouble.'

'That's OK,' I shrugged. 'Thank you for letting me borrow your broomstick, even though you risked getting into trouble for it.'

'Pleasure,' said Lavinia, with a smile. 'Today I've learned that some things are *worth* getting into trouble for!'

I laughed, and Lavinia laughed, too. Her eyes looked sparkly again like they had when we did the potion.

Then I found myself asking her something that I never thought I would ask. *Ever.*

'Do you want to come back to my house, Lavinia? You can call your mum to

tell her from the crystal ball. We can work
on the project together!'

Lavinia looked at me, surprised, and
for a moment I was worried she might say
no. But then she grinned at me.

'I'd love to!' she said. 'That sounds
like fun. Thanks for asking me, Mirabelle!'

We got onto our broomsticks and
rose into the air, heading into the bright
blue sky, towards home. Together.

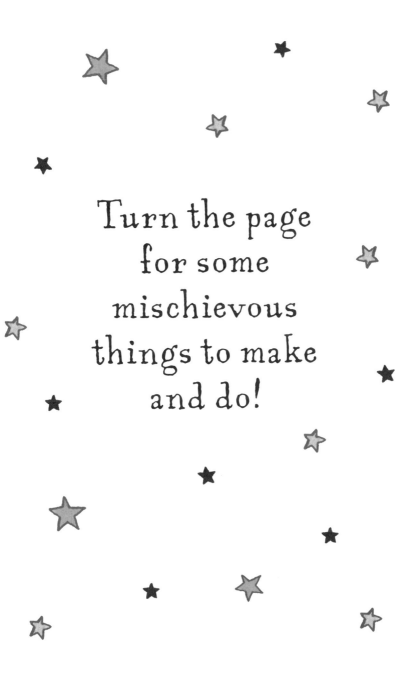

Turn the page
for some
mischievous
things to make
and do!

How to make cupcake-case butterflies!

What you will need:

- A pack of plain white paper cupcake cases
- Pipe cleaners
- Paint

Method:

1. Take a cupcake case and spread it flat.

2. Paint your cupcake case with your favourite colours.
   (Remember to protect your table with e.g. newspaper so it doesn't get messy!)

3. Paint some more cases – you could create a different pattern on each one.

4. Let your cupcake cases completely dry.

5. Pinch your cupcake case in the middle—it will look a bit like a bow, or a pair of butterfly wings!

6. Fold a pipe cleaner in half and place it around your cupcake case wings. This will be the butterfly's body. The two ends of the pipe cleaner should be pointing up, to form its antennae.

7. Twist the pipe cleaner around at the top, to make it secure.

8. Fold out the wings.

9. If your antennae are looking a little long, you could curl them around at the ends.

10. Keep making butterflies until you have a whole family!

You could even use a short length of pipe cleaner to attach a butterfly to a hairclip, just like Mirabelle's in the story. Just don't go out in the rain wearing it, as it won't last long!

Quiz! Which magical creature would you like to meet?

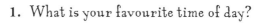

Take the quiz to find out!

1. What is your favourite time of day?

A. I love the night, when the moon is out.

B. I love the morning, when I'm full of energy.

C. I love the evening, just before bedtime when everything feels cosy.

2. What is your favourite game?

A. I like running games, like tag.

B. I like playing rough and tumble games.

C. I like to play hide and seek.

3. What superpower would you choose?

A. Being able to run really fast.

B. Being able to fly.

C. Being invisible.

Results

Mostly As

You would get on well with a moon unicorn!
You could feed them some snafflegrass and watch
them run in the moonlight.

Mostly Bs

Just like Mirabelle, you would like the bittens!
These mischievous creatures are great fun to play
with, just make sure you have a butterfly in case
you need to distract them!

Mostly Cs

You would like to see the giant spiders!
These huge creatures are very elegant, just look
out for the fangs!

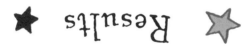

Read more of
Mirabelle's
exciting antics
with Mirabelle
Has a Bad Day

Chapter ONE

'Wheeee!'

It was late-afternoon and I was busy
practising my loop the loops in the garden
before dinner. Flying on my broomstick
is one of my favourite things to do! I love
swooping and swirling and feeling the
wind whirl through my hair.

'Mirabelle!' called Mum from inside.

'It's dinner time! Dad's made fairy meringue pie for pudding!'

'Ooh!' I said excitedly and immediately flew back towards the ground, landing on the grass with a skid.

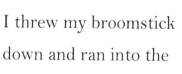

I threw my broomstick
down and ran into the
house with my little dragon
Violet flapping along behind me.

'Did you bring your broomstick in?'
asked Mum as I sat down at the table.

'Oops no,' I said. 'But I promise I'll
fetch it after dinner!'

'As long as you do!' said Mum.
'Broomsticks don't like being left out in
the cold and it's going to rain tonight.'

But by the time dinner was finished
I had forgotten all about my broomstick.
Mum had bought me a new book and I
wanted to read it straightaway. As soon
as the fairy meringue pie was finished

I ran up to my bedroom and snuggled down with Violet to read. The book was *very* good—about a witch who invented a potion that could make your hair turn into sparkling strands of tinsel! I LOVED the idea of tinselly hair! And there was a list of ingredients at the back of the book so you could make the potion yourself! I jumped off my bed before I had even finished the story and collected up all the things I would need, including my travel-size cauldron and laid them on my pillow.

'Mirabelle,' said Mum, poking her head around the door. 'It's past your bedtime!'

'What?!' I had been reading for so long that I hadn't noticed it had got dark outside.

'I just want to make one quick potion Mum before bed. Look, I've already got the ingredients ready!'

Mum glanced at my pillow and frowned.

'Your pillow is not the correct place for potion ingredients,' she said. 'Make sure you clear them up before getting into bed. And there's no time to make the potion now. It's already twenty minutes past your bedtime.'

'Ohhh kaaay,' I sighed. The potion would have to wait for tomorrow. I got changed into my pyjamas, brushed my teeth, and snuggled down into bed to finish my new book by wand light.

I don't use my fairy wand much—witch magic is much more interesting, but it is useful as a torch sometimes. Mum and Dad came in to kiss me goodnight.

'I thought I told you to put your potion ingredients away,' said Mum. 'You can't sleep with them on your pillow like that!'

'I won't,' I promised. 'I just haven't got round to it yet. I'll do it as soon as I've finished this chapter.'

'OK,' said Mum, raising her eyebrows. 'Well make sure you do!' Then she bent down and kissed me goodnight before leaving the room.

I yawned and continued to read my

book, feeling all cosy and cuddly with
Violet.

*'The witch flew across the sky, her silver hair
streaming out behind her like a shooting star.
People down below . . .'*

I yawned again and closed my eyes just
for a moment. It was so comfy lying in
my bed all snuggled with Violet. I could
see the sparkling witch behind my eyelids
now, leaving streaky twinkling trails
in the darkness . . . luring me into the
velvety blackness of sleep.

Harriet Muncaster

Harriet Muncaster, that's me! I'm the
author and illustrator of two young fiction
series, Mirabelle and Isadora Moon.
I love anything teeny tiny, anything
starry, and everything glittery.

Love Mirabelle?
Why not try these too...